Holy Shitballs, You're Awesome!
Volume 1



Published by Iron Pirate Publishing


Printed in the United States



Design by Kathryn Zeigler
Edited by Todd Zeigler & Todd Zeigler

Iron Pirate Publishing
With Special Thanks to Wolfe Creative Solutions

ironpiratepublishing@gmail.com

@ironpiratepublishing
#ironpiratepublishing

For DJ Mom Slice, Princess Pretty Cap, Binkey Blue Eyes, Tiffany Epiphany, the Ewancorn, and Nate Dawg.

Thank you for being cool about the big shoes I fill being of the clown variety.

Fuck. Yes.

Good to see you, bestie.

I want you to do something for me. Right now
And every day before you even pick this
Inspirational Good Book of You
up.

Every morning when those beautiful
(insert color here)
Eyes open.

Repeat the following:

"Let's fuckin' do this."
Learn it. Live it. Love it.

Like I said. Like you said.

Let's fuckin' do this.

Whose voice are you reading this in?

You know, how when you see a famous quote,
You tend to read it in that person's voice?

Whose voice are you reading this in?

Practice it being yours, because you
Should be the biggest fucking cheerleader you have,

You beautiful son of a bitch.

Perfection is not the goal.

Authenticity is.

If nothing else,
It really refines the list
Of people you need to give a fuck about.

I got a crack in my windshield on the goddamn
Interstate today. Wrote your name on it.

That fucker healed right up.

You are an inspiration.

Bet you didn't know I knew Lithuanian.

What's that?

That wasn't Lithuanian?

Fuck - your Lithuanian is way better than mine!

I'm gonna let you in on a secret.

Awkward silence is stupid.

Everyone is waiting for that person
Who will free them to be themselves.

Do it. Be bold.

Free those fuckin' rodeo clowns.

Let them be themselves.

They will love you for it.

Talking with you
Is like being let loose
In the front room of a Cracker Barrel With a gift certificate that says,

"Your money's no good here. Go apeshit."

Don't know if you're a football fan,
But I was at a game the other day.

The referees use Instant Replay
To make sure they get calls right.

I got a peek at their monitor.

It just says
"What would (Your Name) do?"

They nailed every call.

Fucking brilliance, mon frere.

Inside you are two wolves.

Fuck.

That's it.

That's the message.

You have two wolves inside of you.

Wolves are badass, you badass.

Did you hear that asshole?

That one. Over there.

Called you a
(insert your genitalia here.)

(Well, metaphorically.)

Asshole's been talking shit about you.
Pfft. Who cares?

Shit's the only thing
Assholes produce.

(Your genitalia, plural)? They make LIFE. my friend.

Chris Cornell's voice in the last chorus
Of "Show Me How to Live."
That's your whole fuckin' vibe.

Not a rock fan? Um...

The key change in "I Wanna Dance with Somebody."

Shit, you are epic.

Don't just stop and smell the roses today.

Eat some fucking daffodils
In front of your boss.

MAKE THEM SEE YOU.

A smart man once told me how he handles it
When life turns shitty.

He asks himself two questions:

Is anyone going to die?
Is anyone going to jail?

If the answer to both of those questions is "No,"

Calm. The Fuck. Down.

You're so awesome
That when you play board games,
The game says "Sorry!" to you
And all your pieces slide to the Finishing space.

Even when you're not playing "Sorry!"

Fucking Ouija shit, man.

*making spooky fingers*

Just got back from the Louvre.

Stole the fuckin' Mona Lisa.

How'd I get away with it?

I replaced it with your profile picture
And nobody knew the difference.

You work of fucking art.

I’m wearing stilts right now

And I still fuckin' look up to you.

I was tied to railroad tracks
Like in an old-timey western.

Just as I was about to be crushed,
I spoke your name.

The train grew arms and untied me.

Fuck.
Thanks.

That was a close one.

Remember.

You are under no obligation
To take shit from anybody.

And the only shit you should give?

The view inside your asshole
As you rip a fart
In the direction of your haters
And walk away.

You are so cool
That firefighters climb the ladder
And just tell the fire about you.

How's that for sucking the air
Outta the fucking room?

You're so awesome,
"Y" finally made up its damn mind
Whether it's a vowel or not.

Hmm?
Oh.

It's THE vowel.

Air drum solo!

Go!

Holy shit. You're good.

I heard that the stairs in your house
Are so eager to take you downstairs,
They fight their way up to you.

Your house manifested an escalator.

Holy shitballs, you're awesome.

Be the person you needed when you were younger.

If that means buying a Batman costume,
Then fuck it,
Buy a Batman costume.

Do something for me.

Might be a little weird, but go with me.

Hold me to your chest.

Yeah.

That's a motherfuckin' hug,
My friend.

Don't nobody give 'em Like you.

Took a trip to the Rock n Roll Hall of Fame.

I snuck onstage and just screamed
Your name over and over
Into the microphone.

Long story short,
Six bands hired you
And you start Monday.

Fucking hands in the air,
Where you descended from like an angel,
You fucking rock god.

Assholes are going to talk about you.

Who cares?

THEY are talking about YOU.
The power you have.

The free rent
In someone else's head.

Bask in it, you beautiful tattoo
On the chest of LIFE.

FREE SPACE!

Write your own affirmation here!

Use as much profanity as you want!

TREAT YOURSELF!

Follow-up:

Okay,
So it may have felt weird giving yourself an affirmation.

We're trained in this weird-ass culture to humble ourselves.

To dissemble our own self-worth.

That feeling good about
Ourselves is pompous and egomaniacal.

What the actual tap-dancing fuck?

How utterly unhealthy.

There's nothing wrong with feeling good about yourself.

Just have a little
Perspective.

Here's a little perspective: the universe, the moment you live in, is incomprehensibly vast.

Huge.

But it is incomplete without
You.

When you turn my pages,
It's like scratching a dog behind the ear.

Holy shit, that feels good.

You're so awesome,
I heard that when you walk past
The Hall of Presidents,
All the animatronics come to life.

They could rise up in a free-for-all
Of undead executive bedlam,
But they've vowed to stay there
And play their parts out of respect
For the office.

Man.

Performing miracles and preserving democracy.

Holy shitballs, you're awesome.

You know that old tradition in weddings, where the
minister says "If anyone here has any reason
Why these two should not be married…"?

They mention you by name.

Like "Of course, we all know about you-know-who…"

Some people take it as a joke.

But it's really more of a superstition.

Like a banishing spell.

And fucking look at you,

Being all nice and letting them think it's working.

You know what?

Write your name in the front of this.

Like a library book.

"This book belongs to…"

That way, in case you're ever on a rapidly
disintegrating hang glider
(Calm your boobs, you have a parachute)
And this book falls out of the sky and
Whacks someone in the head,
They'll be pleasantly surprised and have you to thank.

How 'bout them balls?

You’re so awesome,
You should give breathing lessons.

Fuck yeah, I know the body does it automatically.

You still do it better.

It's like you're made from the parts
Of lesser unicorns.

You are not the main character
In anyone's story.

Barely yours.

Fucking sucks, right?

So, instead of worrying about that bullshit,
Be a beloved guest star
In as many as possible.

Did you know there has only been
One perfect game in World Series history?

Legend has it that on the first pitch,
When the catcher signaled to the pitcher what to throw,
He spelled your name in ASL.

The rest is history.

Shitballs history.

Lose your earbuds?

Fuck it.

Listen to your music anyway.

Crank that shit up.

If anyone complains,
Tell them it's the
Soundtrack to your life,
And you always have to be prepared
To walk away from an explosion
Like a badass.

Ever look in the mirror and think
"Fuck, I'm ugly"?

Ever stop and think that the you
In the mirror
Is literally backwards?

You are thinking of yourself in a backwards way.

It's nature's greatest "fuck you"
To our mental health
That the one thing we cannot see…
Is ourselves.

You are fucking majestic.

Remember that.

Everyone's heard about
The bullshit number of habits
Of the highly successful
Or whatever.

No one talks about the
13 Nervous Ticks of
People Who Get Shit Done Anyway
And Don't Subscribe to
Others' Definition of Success?

By You.

Okay.

I'll admit this one was hard to come up with today.

But those days happen.

Remember: when all around you Feels like chaos,
IT'S NOT YOU
You are not the craziness.

You are rubbernecking
In a feces hurricane
Against your will.

Stuck in a hurricane?

Be the eye.

The eye of fucking
SAURON,
Baby.

You know how you're supposed to
Talk to your plants because
It helps them grow?

Coffee farmers talk to their beans
About the privilege of coasting
Past your pearlescent chompers,
Down the alabaster sheath of your esophagus,
Into the marble opulence that is your colon.

Strongest.

Damn.

Coffee.

Ever.

Weight-loss-shits-level
Diuretic.

The mere mention of you is a health plan.

Was eating a Double Stuf Oreo.

Accidentally dropping the icing half
On another icing half
I was going to eat next.

Made a Quadruple Stuf Icing Sandwich.

Reminded me of you.

Holy shit.

You're so badass today it's making me kind of Self-conscious.

This one's for your mental health day.

This one's for the days when you're just numb.

When everything feels pointless.

When you just don't feel good enough and like
Nothing will ever get better.

When the world feels empty.

A perspective from the outside:

First of all, it's okay.

There is nothing wrong with you for feeling this way.

The world can seem utterly hopeless and indifferent
Sometimes.

But I promise you: that feeling is the world stopping,
Turning the volume down,
Taking it easy on you,
And waiting until you feel okay.

It's not indifferent.

It's keeping vigil.

We're here for you.

Take your time.

You're so awesome,
You got Billy Corgan
To calm the fuck down
And just carve a damn pumpkin This year.

Happy Halloween.

Did you know if you took
Two copies of this book apart
And sewed the pages together,
You'd have a twin size blanket
Of positivity?

Go ahead, I don't mind.

Knock your nuts off.*

Indulge.

*(That's not an actual expression?

Fuck it.

Make it one.

Trailblaze.)

You're so fucking awesome
That when you accidentally get song lyrics wrong,
The artist has a sudden epiphany,
Says to themselves
"Why didn't I think of that?!"
And re-records it with your words.

But they don't release it
Out of sheer embarrassment.

Bitches.

Walt Disney's birthday is December 5.

Every year, he'd ask
if you'd been born yet.

Yes, you.

By name.
Everyone wondered who the fuck
He was talking about.

He's probably spinning in his grave he
Never got to make a movie about you, With you.

Do me a favor.

Tear this page out and sign the back.

Mail it to me.

Sweet!

Free autograph for being the second member of
Your fan club.

Who's #1?

You are,
Motherfucker.

Did you know there's no mention
Of Jesus smiling in the Bible?

He smiles when he thinks of you.

But there just aren't any words
For what you mean to him.

On December 25,
You will open a present to yourself.

It's this book.

Merry Fuckin' Christmas to you, you absolute gift.

It’s me.

From the beginning of the book.

The Leap Day Bonus page.

I missed you so much,
I tore myself out and moved back here
To see you again.

That one about stilts wasn’t happy about it.

Anyway, hi :).

So here we are.

The end of the year.

It's been a nut-busting pleasure.

I hate to see you go...
Hold on a hot-damn minute.

Time is a circle,
Your time is a hula hoop,
And your hips can fuckin' go, baby!

Turn this fuckin' Good Book of You back to Page 1!

Quick!

See you there!

Holy shitballs. You're awesome.

www.ingramcontent.com/pod-product-compliance
Lightning Source LLC
LaVergne TN
LVHW052103160826
845678LV00015B/3335

* 9 7 9 8 3 6 7 4 3 1 1 4 8 *